CONTENTS

Skate World

Drop down the ramp and feel gravity suck at your stomach as the slope levels out. Pop an **ollie** up on to a rail and grind along it – SCREEECH! Drop back to the ground, give the board a couple of pumps, and head for the next ramp. Welcome to the terrific, terrifying, thrilling world of skateboarding.

DREAM (SKATE) TICKET

Imagine you could go skating anywhere in the world! Where would you go? Where are the best skate spots Planet Earth has to offer? This book will help you decide. Whether you're a beginner, trying to improve, or a full-on expert, we can tell you where to head for.

THE SECRET LANGUAGE OF SKATING

ollie skateboard jump or aerial
poser someone who thinks they're better than they are
trucks devices that connect the deck to the wheels, and allow the board to turn

Andy Macdonald goes for a sunset aerial over a big ramp.

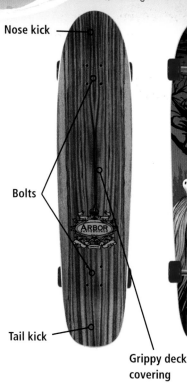

A typical longboard skateboard.

Nose kick

Bolts

ARBOR

Tail kick

Grippy deck
covering

Wheels (big and soft
for smooth rolling)

Truck

Truck bolt

Rubbers (soft for swooping turns)

HINTS AND TIPS

Of course, when you get to the world's best skate spots, you'll need to be sure you know what you're doing. No one wants to look like a **poser**! So we also tell you what to expect at each skate spot, the kind of gear you'll need, tips from local skaters, and advice on techniques. This book is your passport to the skating world!

Technical: Main types of skating

People have been coming up with different uses for their skateboards ever since someone first screwed roller skate wheels to the bottom of an old plank:

Street, park, ramp	Cruising	Speed	Slalom
Each uses basically the same kind of board: a short deck, with a kick (upturn) at the nose and tail; and small, hard wheels.	A long deck – called a longboard – with softer wheels (good for smooth rolling) allows you to cruise around in a mellow style.	Similar to longboard decks, but with harder wheels and less flex in the **trucks**, to prevent speed wobble.	Shorter decks, soft wheels, lots of flex in the trucks for wiggling and waggling through the slalom cones.

Stapelbäddsparken

In Malmö in summer, the sun barely sets. It's still light at midnight – which can make it hard to get to sleep. Even so, if you stumbled across Stapelbäddsparken, you might think you'd fallen asleep and were having a wonderful dream. This place is a skater's idea of heaven.

STAPELBÄDDSPARKEN
Location: Malmö, Sweden
Type of skating: park, ramp
Difficulty level: 1.5 of 5
Best season: June to September

WHY STAPELBÄDDSPARKEN?

The skatepark offers an amazing experience – in summer, at least. Around midsummer the sun sets at 11 p.m. and rises again at 3 a.m. It never really gets dark, and in theory you could skate all night.

On top of the unusual experience, the skating at Stapelbäddsparken is out of this world. The park – which opened in 2006 – covers 2000 square metres (21 500 square feet). Skaters designed the park's bowls, pools, ramps and stairs, and every visiting rider will find something here to amuse them.

Stapelbäddsparken plays host to some of the biggest competitions of the skateboarding year.

THE SECRET LANGUAGE OF SKATING

flatland type of trick skating on flat concrete
run continuous skating time

Regular or goofy?

WHAT TO RIDE

Beginners: Complete beginners would be best starting on the **flatland** area, which would be a great place to work out the basics of skateboarding.

Improvers: Practically the whole park has opportunities for improvers!

Experts: The Ultrabowl, a kidney-shaped pool, challenges even pro riders to put in a good **run**.

One of the first things you have to work out when you start skateboarding is whether you ride regular or goofy.

1. Stand on the deck of the board, facing a handrail or chain-link fence. It needs to be something you can pull yourself along on.

2. Pull yourself in the direction of your left foot for a few metres.

3. Change direction and pull yourself to the right. Repeat this a few times until you can decide which one feels more natural.

4. If you are more comfortable with your left foot in front, you ride regular. If right-foot-forward feels better, you are probably a goofy foot.

Regular riders usually push off with their back foot, while goofy riders push off with their front one.

This skater rides goofy (right foot at the front of the deck).

Tip from a Local

Malmö has other skateparks to try: Sibbarp and Bryggeriet are both smaller, but also great fun.

Woodward West

Woodward is the world's most famous residential camp for skaters. Over the years, thousands of skaters have stayed at Woodward for a week or two each summer, returning home to amaze their friends (and annoy their enemies) with a whole new bag of tricks. Woodward West also opens for a Winter Camp between Christmas and New Year.

WOODWARD WEST
Location: California, USA
Type of skating: all types
Difficulty level: 1–5 of 5

WHY WOODWARD?

Woodward is great for riders of any ability. Beginners get to master the basis of skateboarding incredibly quickly, because they can spend all day, every day practising. Expert riders get the chance to ride an amazing variety of ramps, bowls, and street. Best of all, many of the coaches at Woodward are pro skaters, ready to hand on tricks and tips.

A graduating class at Woodward shows what they've got in an end-of-term exam.

Tip from a Local

Get ready for some heat – the camp is near the Mojave Desert, and temperatures top 38° Centigrade (100° Fahrenheit) in summer.

WHAT TO RIDE

Woodward is definitely somewhere to ride a street/ramp deck. A longboard would make the pools and ramps very hard work!

Indoor skating: Woodward's giant Hangar skatepark offers all skaters a chance to work on their skills. Rails, ramps, bowls and **vert ramps** in a variety of sizes make this a fantastic all-weather skate spot.

Outdoor skating: When the Californian sun cools down, experts head outside to The Crater to show off their bowl-riding skills.

If you like Woodward West...

... you could also try:
- Camp Woodward, USA: more of the same, only in Pennsylvania, USA – and without the Wild West ghost town theme.
- Atlantic Beach Skatelab, Florida, USA for the indoor-skating experience.

THE SECRET LANGUAGE OF SKATING

vert ramp a half-pipe ramp (two ramps linked by a flat section) with vertical sides

stance how you stand on the board

SKILL
Beginner tips

There are a few crucial basic technique tips in skateboarding. It pays to learn these well, as they make more impressive tricks easier.

This girl shows a nice, relaxed style as she gets her board up to speed.

- Stay loose on the board: relax your arms and legs. Most important of all – BEND YOUR KNEES! A straight-up **stance** makes it impossible to learn tricks.

- Place your feet over the truck bolts, or perhaps your back foot slightly behind the rear bolt.

- Practise getting the board up to speed until you can do it without thinking. Start by just pushing off once, then coasting to a stop. Then add in a second push just before you stop. Soon you will feel able to make longer and longer pushes to increase your speed.

Stoke Plaza

Stoke Plaza is a typical local skatepark. Designed by skaters working with the local council, it was built in an area where skating was already popular. This is a place where kids learning to do simple ollies rub shoulders with skaters grinding rails and doing triple **stair jumps**.

STOKE PLAZA
Location: Staffordshire, England
Type of skating: park, ramp
Difficulty level: 2 of 5
Best season: May to September

WHY STOKE PLAZA?

At over 3000 square metres (32 300 square feet), Stoke Plaza is one of the biggest skateparks in the UK – and, for that matter, Europe. It is near to some of the country's biggest cities, so there's rarely a quiet day here. Skaters come from all around to ride at the Plaza, and they include some real experts. There's bound to be someone you can watch and learn from.

THE SECRET LANGUAGE OF SKATING

stair jump ollie (sometimes a big one) down a flight of stairs

SKILL
Stopping

Whatever kind of skating you're into, the second thing you need to learn is how to stop. (The first thing is how to go, obviously.) This is a simple way to slow down or stop a skateboard.

1. Start by riding along at a not-too-fast speed. Remember to keep both knees bent all the time.

2. Put your back foot flat on the floor, but forwards of where it naturally goes. It should be almost beside your front foot.

3. Let your foot drag gently backwards, then lift it and place it back where it began.

With a bit of practice, this technique becomes automatic, making skating safer for you, the skater, as well as passers-by.

Tip from a Local
If you want a rest, head for one of the Safe Zones, where you can watch the action without getting in anyone's way.

A nice grind along the coping at Stoke Plaza.

An overview of the Stoke Plaza Skatepark.

WHAT TO RIDE

The park is a street-skating location. The paths nearby would be OK for cruising on a longboard, but that's not why you would visit Stoke.

Beginners: Most beginners will stick to the street area, where there are obstacles small enough to start learning simple tricks on – without getting badly hurt if they go wrong.

Improvers and experts: The street area has plenty of things to interest experts, but they will also want to try their hand in the bowl.

If you like Stoke...
... you could also try:
• Marseille Skatepark, France
• Riverslide Skatepark, Australia
Both offer a modern urban skating experience.

Kona Skatepark

Skating has a long history in Florida. Some people say that this is where the world's first outdoor skatepark was built, in 1976. Not long after this the Kona Skatepark opened. Amazingly, Kona still has some of its original runs – as well as plenty of new attractions.

KONA SKATEPARK
Location: Florida, USA
Type of skating: park, ramp
Difficulty level: 2 of 5
Best season: all year

Riding the Kona snake run.

Tip from a Local

You have to wear a helmet at Kona, plus wrist guards, elbow and knee pads if you're under 16.

The legendary (and very nicely painted) Kona Skatepark in Florida.

If you like Kona...

... you could also try:
- Southsea Skatepark, England
- Parque da Marina, Porto Allegre, Brazil

They both have great old-school snake runs.

Why Kona?

If you travel to Kona you'll be following in famous footsteps. Tony Hawk says that, "Kona was the first place I ever travelled to, at 12, as a sponsored amateur skater." One of the things Hawk still loves about Kona is the old **snake run**. Only a few of these still exist, so the chance to ride one is a rare opportunity.

THE SECRET LANGUAGE OF SKATING

snake run downhill speed run with banked turns

pool deck slightly longer and wider than a modern deck, with less nose flip and a square tail. Used with softer wheels.

What to ride

This is a place where you could happily bring an old-style **pool deck** and have a LOT of fun. Of course, a modern street deck would also be fine.

Improvers: It's impossible to hang out at Kona for more than an hour without giving the snake run and the old 1970s pools a go.

Experts: The old 25-metre (82-foot) wide vert ramp and the two new street-skating courses will provide hours and hours of entertainment.

SKILL
Slalom

Recently, old-school skateboarding has become increasingly popular. One side of this is the growing number of longboard and pool decks. Another is the rise in slalom competitions.

• The runs are usually on flat land, with sets of cones set out in a line with an equal gap between each cone.

• Sometimes two runs are side-by-side; otherwise, the runs are timed.

• The riders start by pumping for as much speed as possible. They weave between the cones without hitting any all the way down the course.

• The best technique is to have bent knees (of course) and use your hips to swing the board in and out of the cones. It's important to get a rhythm, or you quickly start hitting cones. Sometimes it's better to go slower and be accurate!

Traffic stops on a side street to allow this slalom contest to take place. Note the start ramps, which help the competitors to pick up a decent amount of speed.

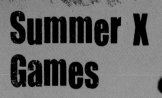

Summer X Games

Shaun White gets airborne in the vert event at the 2009 X Games.

SUMMER X GAMES
Location: Los Angeles, USA
Type of skating: park, vert
Difficulty level: 5 of 5
Takes place: usually in August

The X Games is the world's biggest extreme-sports event. It's a bit like an annual Olympic Games for skateboarding, BMX, motocross, and other hard-charging sports. The winners compete for gold, silver and bronze medals. There is also prize money, as well as the chance to be seen on an international sports TV channel (the games are sponsored by a TV company).

If you like X Games...
… you could also try:
• Dew Tour events
• Tony Hawk's Boom Boom
  Huck Jam Tour

SKATEBOARDING AT THE X GAMES

The skating contests that draw the biggest crowds at the Games are the **Big Air** and the vert ramp competitions. The street contest is almost as popular.

The X Games are known for being the place where some famous tricks were performed for the first time. Best known of all, in 1999 Tony Hawk landed a 900 (a 900-degree spin) for the first time – after 11 failed attempts. In 2005, Gabriel Ramos tried to land a 1080 – and failed, 29 times.

THE SECRET LANGUAGE OF SKATING

Big Air event in which competitors try to pull off the biggest jumps they can

Night-time action on the giant X-Games ramp; Andy Macdonald thrills an equally giant crowd of skate fans.

FAMOUS X GAMES COMPETITORS

• **Tony Hawk**: the first skater to land a 900 (see above).
• **Andy Macdonald**: in 2008, he overtook Tony Hawk to become the person who has won the most skateboarding medals, with 15.
• **Shaun White**: the only person to win gold at the Summer X Games (for skateboarding) and the Winter X Games (for snowboarding).
• **Jake Brown**: in 2007, Brown had "the worst fall ever in the X Games", landing on his back from 10 metres (33 feet) in the air. Though seriously injured, he walked away.

Berkeley

The rolling hills of Berkeley have been popular with skaters ever since skateboarding first started. Today there are plenty of places for street and ramp skating, but one of the most popular forms of riding here is a relatively new kind of skating – longboarding.

WHY BERKELEY?

Berkeley is hilly. Not breathtakingly hilly, like San Francisco across the bay, but just right for longboarding. For students at the university campus it is a great way to get around, and there is a lively longboarding scene there. Meanwhile, downhill speed runs take place in the hills above the city.

Tip from a Local

For good park and ramp skating, try the 1600-square-metre (17 200-square-foot) skatepark in Berkeley's Harrison Park.

Tony Alva, one of California's famous Dogtown skate crew, known as the Z-Boys, in 1978.

WHAT TO RIDE

Longboard decks: Most longboard decks are about waist-high to the rider. They are often **concave**, with wide trucks and softer wheels than street decks. For sliding, the wheels are usually a little harder than normal: between 90a and 92a **durometer**.

Other tips: One skateboard braking technique is called a Coleman slide – named after the legendary 1970s Berkeley skater Cliff Coleman.

THE SECRET LANGUAGE OF SKATING

concave deck that curves up towards the edges

durometer how hard a wheel is (lower numbers are softer)

If you like Berkeley ...

... you could also try:
• Brighton, England
• Bilbao, Spain

SKILL
Slide braking

Longboards can travel pretty fast, especially downhill. If there's one skill you really need on a longboard, it's being able to stop quickly.

Part-way through a slide – commit to the turn, or you risk being spat out on to the tarmac.

1. Wear AT LEAST tough gloves, because your hands will scrape on the ground, and a helmet.

2. Practise crouching down on your board at speed. Crouch, stand, crouch again, and keep going until it feels fast and comfortable.

3. Now crouch down and start a hard turn, putting weight into your front foot.

4. Push the back of the board away from you with your rear foot. The rear wheels should slide away.

5. Some people put their front hand on the ground and hold on to the toe edge of the board with their rear hand to help the slide.

Millennium Skatepark

The Millennium Skatepark makes a BIG impression the first time you go there. At over 8000 square metres (86 100 square feet), this is the world's largest outdoor public skatepark. Even better, it's open 24 hours a day, and it's free. If you feel the need to work on your **Mctwists** at 3 a.m., you won't even have to pay to get in.

MILLENNIUM SKATEPARK
Location: Alberta, Canada
Type of skating: park, ramp
Difficulty level: 3 of 5
Best season: June to September

WHY MILLENNIUM?

Millennium is separated into three areas, for beginners, improvers and experts, making it easy to work out which sections will suit you best. There are no requirements for helmets, pads and other safety kit (but leave them unworn at your own risk). In July and August, during the warmest weather, lessons are available.

Sliding the tail along a bench at Millennium

Tip from a Local

A snake run has recently been added at Millennium – one of the first new snake runs for years.

WHERE TO RIDE

Beginners: The Intro Area has low stairs, rails you can roll on to, and banked bowls, all designed to improve skills and confidence.

Improvers: The Central Park has just about every kind of skate feature you can think of, including ramps and street furniture.

Experts: The separate Expert Park has a mouth-watering selection of bowls and pipes – including a 10-metre (33-foot) **full pipe**.

If you like Millennium...

... you could also try:
• Amarillo Skatepark, USA
• Ramp City, Blackpool, England
Both have full pipes.

SKILL
Learn to ollie

An ollie – a hands-free jump, often off a flat surface – is one of the first tricks skaters want to learn, once they have mastered the basic skills.

This board is just about going to level out as it lands on the ground.

1. Put the ball of your back foot on the tail of the board, behind the truck bolts. Keep your knees well bent.

2. Slam your back foot down hard on to the tail and immediately jump into the air. The front of the board will lift up.

3. Roll your front foot against the deck of the board, which will bring the tail up.

4. Pull up your knees as the board levels out.

5. Land flat on the deck, using your knees to absorb the landing, and roll away wearing a big grin.

Amazing Square

Skateboarding is still a new, growing sport in Japan. Because outdoor space is limited in Japanese cities, most skateparks are inside. Amazing Square is unusual for being out in the air – especially in a city as jam-packed with people as Tokyo.

AMAZING SQUARE
Location: Tokyo, Japan
Type of skating: vert ramp, ramp, park
Difficulty level: 3.5 of 5
Best season: all year

WHY AMAZING SQUARE?
The best skatepark in Japan? Possibly. Amazing Square is a wonderful place to skate. The **mini-ramps** and the enormous vert ramp are made of plywood rather than concrete, which gives riding here a special feel. On top of that, the park is open 24 hours a day, so whenever the urge to skate strikes, Amazing Square will be there waiting.

If you like Amazing Square...
... you could also try:
• Benalmadena, Spain
• Livingston, Scotland
Both offer great varied skating.

Night-time fun at the Amazing Square Skatepark in Tokyo, Japan.

THE SECRET LANGUAGE OF SKATING

mini-ramp small version of a vert ramp, without vertical sides

At this point, it's WAY too late to chicken out!

WHAT TO RIDE

This is a place for park and ramp riding, so bring a board set up for that.

Improvers: Mini-ramps, street courses, stairs, rails – this park has everything an improving skater needs.

Experts: The biggest draw for experts will be the giant vert ramp, which towers above the rest of the park.

Other tips: Japanese skaters are probably the most polite in the world. It's important to be polite back.

Tip from a Local

If you want to congratulate a Japanese skater on a good trick, say "*Sugoi!*"

One of the big attractions at Amazing Square is the ramps – especially the huge vert ramp. To ride ramps like this, the first skill you need is to be able to drop in.

1. Set the tail of the deck on the edge of the ramp and stand on it. The front truck will be hanging out into space.

2. Put your front foot over the front trucks. Stomp the front foot down and lean into it as the board drops down the ramp. COMMITMENT RULES here – don't hesitate! Keep your knees bent and your body as compact as possible.

3. Let your knees absorb the transition at the bottom of the ramp. Straighten slightly, but keep them bent, ready to absorb the next transition – up the opposite ramp.

As with all tricks, start small, and work your way up to a bigger ramp bit by bit.

Downhill Skateboarding World Cup

DOWNHILL SKATEBOARDING
WORLD CUP
Location: worldwide
Type of skating: downhill speed
Difficulty level: 4 of 5
Season runs: May to December

Downhill racers tuck into an aerodynamic shape, hoping to squeeze maximum speed out of the course.

This is a skating event with a difference. You won't hear the screech of trucks grinding on rails, or the sudden silence of a ramp rider getting airborne. All you hear is the whoosh of longboards racing down the hill – and possibly a "Whoooah!" once in a while, as a rider loses control on a bend.

THE SECRET LANGUAGE OF SKATING

full face covering head, face and chin

DOWNHILL WORLD CUP
The Downhill World Cup is a series of downhill speed events. The racers compete side-by-side, and the fastest riders stay in the contest until there's a winner. Since 2007, the UK leg of the World Cup has taken place at Beachy Head, Eastbourne, in England. Each year it draws bigger crowds, and more competitors decide to give this unusual kind of skating contest a try.

DOWNHILL EQUIPMENT

If you arrive to watch one of these contests expecting to see the usual skater gear of baggy shorts or jeans, T-shirts and hoodies, you'll get a shock. The racers generally wear motorbike leathers and **full-face** helmets to protect themselves. The boards are long and narrow at the nose and tail, with wide trucks and big wheels.

WORLD CHAMPIONSHIPS

As well as the World Cup, there is a one-off World Championship once a year. The contest changes location, but in 2009 it was held at Bathurst, NSW, Australia.

Tight racing at the UK leg of the Downhill World Cup.

Tip from a Fan

You can find your local Downhill World Cup event at **www.igsaworldcup.com** – click on "Events" and find the results section to see where the most recent races were held.

23

Bay Sixty6

This park used to be called Playstation, but changed its name when Xbox took over sponsorship. Either way, this is a computer-company game with a difference – getting burned here really hurts! The concrete is real, not digital, and you can't pause the action halfway through.

BAY SIXTY6
Location: London, England
Type of skating: park, ramp
Difficulty level: 4 of 5
Best season: all year

If you like Bay Sixty6...

… you could also try:
- Lake Cunningham Skatepark, California, USA

Bay Sixty6 in London is especially busy on rainy days – it's easy to see why.

WHY BAY SIXTY6?

Bay Sixty6 is the only indoor skatepark in London (technically, at least: it's underneath a huge motorway bridge). It's also the only vert ramp in London.

As such, this is where some of the UK's best skaters come to practise and compete. Watch a session here, and you're almost sure to go home inspired to skate harder.

THE SECRET LANGUAGE OF SKATING

vert wall essentially, one half of a vert ramp

Tip from a Local

Call and check the park will be open if you plan on a special visit – it's sometimes closed for demo days or filming.

EQUIPMENT

Beginners: On weekend mornings there's a beginners' session.

Improvers and experts: Bay Sixty6 has too many attractions to list them all. They include a 3.3-metre (10.8-foot) sunken vert ramp, a great 1.8-metre (6-foot) mini-ramp, a huge **vert wall**, and loads of street furniture.

Other tips: If you're going to visit more than five times, it's worth becoming a member: it makes admission cheaper.

Adding a bit of style to an ollie by adding in a nose grab, which is one of the easiest grabs to learn.

SKILL
Ollie off a ramp

Advanced street and ramp-riding tricks sometimes require you to ollie off a ramp. This is essentially the same as a regular ollie: what's different is that you are much higher up. Start small, and steadily build up to higher ramps as you get more confident.

1. Approach the ramp with a fair amount of speed, riding straight at it.

2. Keep your feet in the usual ollie position, shift weight to your back foot as you ride up the ramp.

3. Do a regular ollie as the front wheels are about to hit the lip.

4. Sail through the air.

5. Land, using your knees to absorb the force, before riding away wearing an even BIGGER grin than the one you had after your first flatland ollie (see page 19).

Paris

Most skaters learn in skateparks. You're allowed to skate there (obviously!), so police and security guards don't tell you off. There are lots of different ramps and other obstacles to skate, all packed together in one area. But expert skaters also take to the streets – and there can't be many better places for street skating than Paris.

Skating Paris with one of the city's most famous landmarks, the Eiffel Tower, in the background.

PARIS
Location: Paris, France
Type of skating: street
Difficulty level: 4 of 5
Best season: May to September

Tip from a Local
The 3000-square-metre (32 300-square-foot) Skatepark de Paris, in the 18th Arrondissement, is the biggest skatepark in Paris.

If you like Paris…
… you could also try:
• London, England
• New York, USA
Both offer great street skating for fearless experts.

WHY PARIS?

Paris is one of the oldest cities in Europe. The feeling of history is tremendous, as you skate past pavement cafés and grand old ladies with poodles on leads. To get a sense of what it's like, do an Internet search for the movie *PARISien, version longue*. It features pro skater Soy Panday as he spends a day cruising around the city's streets.

THE SECRET LANGUAGE OF SKATING

waxed covered in wax, to make grinding easier. A waxed concrete edge is a sure sign of a popular skate spot.

WHAT TO RIDE

A street deck is needed for tricks and to skate some of the famous Paris obstacles. For just cruising around, a longboard would be great.

Beginners and improvers: The best place in Paris for beginners and improvers is the Skatepark de Paris.

The beginner area there is called the Zone Débutant.

Experts: Famous street-skating spots in Paris include the stairs and rails at the Cité de Science in La Villette, the concrete wall at La Vague de Clichy/Batignolles, and the **waxed** concrete blocks at Bercy. But there are skate spots all over the city.

Technical: Guidelines for street skating

Street skating is definitely for experts only. With innocent passers-by, bikes, cars and buses around, it would be very dangerous for a trick to go wrong. Even experts need to follow these few guidelines:

• NEVER skate where it's not allowed. It makes people dislike skateboarders, and increases the chances of skating being banned everywhere.

• Always stop skating to let people pass. People often expect skaters to be rude: many become skateboard supporters if they discover this to be wrong.

• Take care not to scare non-skaters. The noise of your wheels makes it sound as if you're nearer than you are – always give people a bit more room than you think is needed.

• Don't push yourself on the street – it's not a good place for learning or perfecting new tricks.

NO SKATEBOARDING

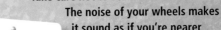

Encinitas YMCA

ENCINITAS YMCA
Location: California, USA
Type of skating: pipe
Difficulty level: 3 to 4 of 5
Best season: all year

Tip from a Local

If you get tired of skating, some of California's most famous surf breaks are nearby – they offer a great way to cool down after a hot skate.

You may not realize it, but if you are at all interested in skateboarding you've probably already seen the Encinitas YMCA. Encinitas is home to one of the most famous vert ramps in history. For years, the ramp has been appearing in DVDs, adverts, posters, photo sessions and magazines.

WHY ENCINITAS YMCA?

It's no surprise that people keep coming back, once they have visited this skatepark. The warm Southern California weather combines with the ramps, bowls and street course to make this a fantastic place to skate. You don't have to want to tackle the vert ramp to take a trip here: there is skating for every level, not only experts.

Whoa, boy! This rider looks unlikely to reconnect with his board on the way down.

WHAT TO RIDE

Beginners and improvers: For beginners, Mini-Land is designed to help build skills. Improvers will want to try the street course and the two cement pools.

Experts: The giant vert ramp is why most experts come to Encinitas to skate. This monster ramp – 25 metres (82 feet) wide, with 4-metre (13-foot) sides and a 6-metre (19.7-foot) **roll-in** – was used for the vert contest at the 2003 X Games.

Other tips: You have to wear a helmet. Under-8s must wear a helmet, knee and elbow pads. Bring your own, because the park doesn't rent them out.

If you like Encinitas YMCA...

... you could also try:
• The Mega Ramp, USA
This became the world's biggest skateboard ramp when it opened in Vista, California.

THE SECRET LANGUAGE OF SKATING

roll-in extension to a vert ramp, allowing greater speed as you drop in

Technical: Pipe etiquette

The first time you launch down any kind of vert ramp or mini-ramp is pretty scary. It's pretty scary for the people around you, too – they really don't want an inexperienced skater crashing into them. So skaters have developed a set of rules for how to behave on a ramp.

• DON'T be a SNAKE. Snakes refuse to wait their turn to have a go. They launch down the ramp and cut across other skaters.

• While waiting your turn, STAND BACK from the top of the ramp. Anything less than a board's length means you might get in the way of whoever is riding at the time.

• Give people a cheer when they land a trick. (A skater version of cheering is to bang the nose or tail of your deck on the metal railing at the top of the ramp. Yelling is allowed too.)

Skaters wait for a turn at the mini-ramp at The Level Skatepark in Brighton, England.

Glossary

WORDS FROM THE SECRET LANGUAGE FEATURES

Big Air event in which competitors try to pull off the biggest jumps they can

concave deck that curves up towards the edges

durometer how hard a wheel is (lower numbers are softer)

flatland type of trick skating on flat concrete

full face covering head, face and chin

full pipe pipe that looks like a circle when seen from the end

Mctwist ramp trick, featuring a 540-degree spin, named after Mike McGill

mini-ramp small version of a vert ramp, without vertical sides

ollie skateboard jump or aerial

pool deck slightly longer and wider than a modern deck, with less nose flip and a square tail. Used with softer wheels.

poser someone who thinks they're better than they are

roll-in extension to a vert ramp, allowing greater speed as you drop in

run continuous skating time

snake run downhill speed run with banked turns

stair jump ollie (sometimes a big one) down a flight of stairs

stance how you stand on the board

trucks devices that connect the deck to the wheels, and allow the board to turn

vert ramp a half-pipe ramp (two ramps linked by a flat section) with vertical sides

vert wall essentially, one half of a vert ramp

waxed covered in wax, to make grinding easier. A waxed concrete edge is a sure sign of a popular skate spot

OTHER WORDS SKATERS USE

brain bucket helmet

carve long, drawn-out turn

coping rounded lip on a ramp or obstacle, usually made of metal or plastic pipe

fakie riding backwards

half pipe another name for a vert ramp

kicker jump ramp, used to get a skater airborne before performing a trick

load up add weight to (usually describing one side of the truck or the other)

spine ramp two half pipes back-to-back, creating a double-U-shaped ramp

street luge contest where riders slide downhill lying on their backs

wipeout crash

Finding Out More

THE INTERNET

www.internationalskateboardingfederation.com
Governing body for skateboarding and organizer of the skateboarding World Championships, the ISF also has links to the X Games, Dew Tour and Adrenalin Games.

www.igsaworldcup.com
The home page of the International Gravity Sports Association, which organizes international downhill skateboarding contests.

www.concretewavemagazine.com
A high-quality skate magazine, both in print and online, which features unusual articles.

http://skateistan.org
Peace through skating – at least, that's what the organizers hope. This is the site of Afghanistan's first skateboarding school, established by foreign volunteer skaters.

BOOKS

Diary of A Skateboarding Freak Ben Powell (Heinemann Library, 2004)
Extracts from the diary of a young man who goes from being a complete skating beginner to the brink of becoming a sponsored rider.

Skateboarding Skills: The Rider's Guide Ben Powell (Firefly Books, 2008)
Written by the editor of *Sidewalk* magazine, this book is an excellent resource for beginner and improver skaters.

Skateboarding: Landing The Basic Tricks Ryan Stutt (A & C Black, 2009)
The author is a keen skater and former editor of the Canadian skateboarding magazine *SBC Skateboarding*. The book tells you everything you need to know to get started and progress as a skater.

MAGAZINES

Sidewalk
Keep up to date with the UK and international skate scene, with articles on skate spots, techniques, personalities, equipment and competition. It also has a good website at **http://sidewalkmag.com**.

Skateboarder
This US magazine has high-quality text and similar content to *Sidewalk*, but obviously from a North American viewpoint. Also has a website at **www.skateboardermag.com**.

Index